SO-DZP-843

An Adequate Education Defined

by
M. Donald Thomas
and
E.E. (Gene) Davis

ISBN 0-87367-676-9
Copyright © 2001 by the Phi Delta Kappa Educational Foundation
Bloomington, Indiana

This fastback is sponsored by the University of South Dakota Chapter of Phi Delta Kappa International, which made a generous contribution toward publication costs.

Table of Contents

Foreword

Historically, court decisions have dealt with "equity"; now they are helping to establish "adequacy" as a standard in education. A number of state supreme courts recently have ruled that education in their states is not financed at an "adequate" level. Legislatures, however, have been slow to enact remedies. In most cases such remedies require states to increase taxes, something they often do not have the courage to do.

What constitutes an adequate education is a complex problem. It requires judicial interpretation of the education clause in a state's constitution and appropriate action by the legislature when mandated by the court's decision. What constitutes adequacy varies from state to state. It also varies with different student demographics and geographic areas within a state.

In the future the U.S. Supreme Court may rule that in a modern, highly literate, technical society, an adequate education is a fundamental right of all children. If that happens, the 14th Amendment to the U.S. Constitution will protect all students from the indifference of politicians.

This fastback is written by two educators who have been heavily involved with school finance issues. Both have worked with state legislative bodies to reform school funding structures. They discuss recent court decisions and present a thorough review of adequacy as it appears in the literature and in court decisions. More important, Thomas and Davis suggest methods that can be used to arrive at an adequate state education finance program.

An Adequate Education Defined is timely and well written. It should be useful to both school leaders and legislators. It also can assist judges as they struggle to define what constitutes an adequate education for all children.

> David V. Thomas, Esquire
> At Counsel
> Alf and Associates
> Las Vegas, Nevada

Introduction

Historically, state supreme courts have been concerned with equity in school financing. They have ruled that state school finance schemes are unconstitutional when there is a wide disparity among school districts in the money available for education. Recently, however, the courts also have attempted to resolve the problem of *adequacy*. Although the courts have stressed that legislative bodies should provide an adequate education, they have not determined what constitutes adequacy.

However, one debate over education adequacy is settled: Our schools are *not* financed at an adequate level. The challenge today is to determine what constitutes an adequate education.

This fastback is divided into three sections. Section one presents the various state supreme court decisions that strongly declare that education in their states is not provided with adequate financial support. Section two presents five methods for establishing adequacy. Section three provides a program for establishing an exemplary adequate finance system for education in any state.

It should be noted that what is "adequate" differs from state to state. These differences are the result of historical practices, geographic value of education, legislative actions, and economic development. For example, what constitutes adequacy in economically depressed states, especially those in the South, may require lower expenditures than in a wealthier state.

We deal with adequacy within the states and not among the states. Currently, each state is struggling with the adequacy question only in terms of itself, not how it compares to other states. The more daunting challenge of adequacy among the states may become more important as the political rhetoric heats up and politicians again trumpet the need to meet "world standards" and "higher levels of student performance."

An Adequate Education Defined is intended as an aid to legislative bodies, state boards of education, and school finance personnel. Establishing financial adequacy for our schools is the right thing to do. As Burrup and his colleagues wrote: "Unfortunately, many of the citizens of this country have never given education the high priority it deserves, requires, and must have if the schools are to accomplish their objectives" (1999, p. 37). It is time for legislative bodies to do what so many courts have said they must do — provide adequate funds for public education.

Court Decisions on Adequacy

The first major case to deal with the issue of adequacy occurred in 1979 in West Virginia. In the case, *Pauley* v. *Kelly*, the court found that West Virginia's school finance system was not adequate in providing facilities, education programs, and services to special education children. In addition, the system created a large disparity between low-wealth and high-wealth school districts (255 S.E.2d 859, W. Va. 1979). Since then, other state supreme courts have made similar rulings.

Although the courts have stressed that legislative bodies should provide an adequate education, they have not determined what constitutes adequacy. One reason is that the courts are not eager to legislate adequacy, a responsibility that belongs to state legislatures. However, the courts have given legislators a few guidelines on what constitutes an adequate education. Following are a few examples:

In 1989 the Kentucky Supreme Court found that the entire education system in that state was unconstitutional. The court stated that an adequate education program should make it possible for students to obtain:

- Sufficient oral and written communication skills to enable students to function in a complex and rapidly changing civilization.
- Sufficient knowledge of economic, social, and political systems to enable the students to make informed choices.
- Sufficient understanding of governmental processes to enable the students to understand the issues that affect their community, state, and nation.
- Sufficient self-knowledge and knowledge of their mental and physical wellness.
- Sufficient grounding in the arts to enable each student to appreciate his or her cultural and historical heritage.
- Sufficient training or preparation for advanced training in either academic or vocational fields so as to enable each child to choose and pursue life work intelligently.
- Sufficient levels of academic or vocational skills to enable public school students to compete favorably with their counterparts in surrounding states, in academics or in the job market (*Rose* v. *Council for Better Education, Inc.*, 790 S.W.2d 186, Ky. 1989).

On 22 April 1999, the South Carolina Supreme Court said that the state constitution "requires the General Assembly to provide the opportunity for each child to receive a minimally adequate education." The court also provided a definition for adequacy:

1. The ability to read, write, and speak the English language, the knowledge of mathematics and physical science.
2. Fundamental knowledge of economic, social, and political systems and of history and governmental process.
3. Academic and vocational skills (*Abbeville et al.* v. *South Carolina*, 335 So. Ca., S.C. 58, 1999).

This decision, written by Chief Justice Ernest Finney Jr., follows similar supreme court decisions in several other states, which also have found that education is not financially supported at an adequate level. The decisions have the primary purpose of assisting legislators to establish an education system that is fair for all children, legally justifiable, morally needed, and adequately financed.

Some other decisions that have attempted to define adequacy are:

Supreme Court of Wyoming. The court said that the constitution required "a thorough and efficient system of public schools, adequate to the proper instruction of all youth of the state." The court also stated that education must be "adequate to prepare students for college admission" (*Campbell County Sch. Dist.* v. *Ohman*, 907 P.2d 1238. Wyo. 1995).

Supreme Court of Ohio. In noting that many schools had pupil-teacher ratios of more than 30 students per classroom, the court said: "As the testimony of educators established, it is virtually impossible for students to receive an adequate education with a student-teacher ratio of this magnitude" (*DeRolph* v. *State*, 677 N.E.2nd 733, Ohio 1997).

Supreme Court of Texas. The court defined adequacy as a "general definition of knowledge." It also stated that "the amount of money spent on a student's education has a real and meaningful impact on the educational opportunity offered to that student" (*Edgewood Indep. Sch. Dist.* v. *Meno*, 893 S.W.2d 450, Tex. 1995).

Supreme Court of New Hampshire. The court said:

> We look to the seven criteria articulated by the Supreme Court of Kentucky as establishing general, aspirational guidelines for defining educational adequacy. A constitutionally adequate public education should reflect consideration of the following:
>
> (i) sufficient oral and written communication skills to enable students to function in a complex and rapidly changing civilization;
>
> (ii) sufficient knowledge of economic, social, and political systems to enable the student to make informed choices;
>
> (iii) sufficient understanding of governmental process to enable the student to understand the issues that affect his or her community, state, and nation;
>
> (iv) sufficient self-knowledge and knowledge of his or her mental and physical wellness;
>
> (v) sufficient grounding in the arts to enable each student to appreciate his or her cultural and historical heritage;
>
> (vi) sufficient training or preparation for advanced training in either academic or vocational fields so as to enable each child to choose and pursue life work intelligently; and

(vii) sufficient levels of academic or vocational skills to enable public school students to compete favorably with their counterparts in surrounding states, in academics or in the job market. (*Claremont Sch. Dist.* v. *Governor*, 703 A.2nd 1353, N.H. 1997).

Supreme Court of Alabama. The Alabama Supreme Court was the most aggressive in defining an adequate education. It articulated nine items that constitute "adequate educational opportunities." The items range from "sufficient oral and written communication skills" to living up to one's "full human potential." The court ordered that "state officers" provide "equitable and adequate educational opportunities to all school-age children, including children with disabilities" (*Joyce Pinto et al.* v. *Alabama Coalition for Equity et al.*, 662 So. 2nd 894, Ala. 1995).

An adequate education is not a legal theory. Rather, it is a judicial interpretation. Such interpretation varies from state to state. One of the authors, while working with a legislative body, was asked what it would take to improve education results in the state. Given the money required, one of the legislators said, "I'm satisfied with the current levels of achievement." The average graduate was reading at a fourth-grade level.

Adequacy also is aligned to the state constitution's education clause. Some are more explicit than others in assisting the courts to define what is an adequate education, especially in establishing adequacy for facilities, education programs, and services to special needs children.

The courts can direct legislative bodies to establish adequacy but have no enforcing powers to see that adequacy is, in fact, established. Legislative bodies may present the courts with proposed solutions, which the courts may accept or reject.

These various court decisions make it clear that the vision of the justices far exceeds that of legislators when it comes to defining an adequate education for all children. The courts also are more realistic than legislative bodies in linking expenditure levels with adequacy. To the courts, money does make a difference; and adequacy requires a substantially higher expenditure, especially for low-wealth school districts.

Recently in Ohio, Senate President Richard Finan is quoted as saying: "This should run up the flag for our friends in wealthier districts. It raises the head of redistribution" (Ludlow 2000). This is exactly what the court had ordered — school district financial support based on the entire wealth of the state. Rather than supporting the court order, Finan attempted to evade it.

Unfortunately, the directives of the courts often are ignored by legislators, and it sometimes requires a decade or more to correct the unconstitutional practices of the state. Long and protracted debate has occurred in California, Texas, Ohio, New Jersey, and many other states. One wonders why the moral responsibility of establishing education adequacy for our children is such a demonic burden for our legislators to accept. The courts have been requesting and directing legislators to provide the necessary funds for a long time.

Financial Theories on Adequacy

Once adequacy is defined, the more complex challenge is one of determining the level of funding that should be provided. School funding experts have devised a number of funding schemes, some rather simple and others based on extremely complicated mathematical computations. Table 1 on the next page shows one suggested funding scheme as applied to "School District X." State funds are distributed on the basis of weighted pupil units (WPUs). The total number of WPUs is established by multiplying membership by appropriate weightings and adding all categories to obtain a total number of students.

Although consultants in this area differ in establishing adequacy, all theoretical approaches have these elements in common:

- Each non-weighted student in the state receives an equal amount of dollars. The amount is usually based on the cost of educating a regular fourth-

Table 1. A suggested funding scheme for financing an adequate education in each school district.

School District X: 1,000 Students, Base Student Cost of $5,400.

Student Numbers	Category	Base Cost	Weight Index	Total Allocation
80	Reg. Grade 4	$5,500	None	$ 440,000
300	High School	5,500	1.08	1,782,000
200	Poverty	5,500	1.25	1,375,000
100 Sp. Ed.				
3	Autistic	5,500	4.0	66,000
97	Various Disabilities	5,500	1.5	800,250
50	Gifted	5,500	1.5	412,500
10	Special Needs	5,500	1.75	96,250
260	Non-Weighted	5,500	None	1,430,000
		State Funds		$6,402,000

Urban District Overburden $1.10 \times 6,402,000 = 7.042,200$ Total State Funds

Transportation 100% Funding of Approved Routes

Facilities 100% Funding Based on Need

Average Expenditure Per Pupil is $7,042.20

Total Number of Weighted Pupil Unit is $1,280.40

1,280.40 WPUs x $5,500 = $7,042,200

In addition to these basic costs, the state may also fund categorical programs, research efforts, and competitive grants, which it believes to be in the state's interest. Separate funds are allocated for buildings and for transportation.

grade student. This is commonly called "the foundation program."

- The base student cost (cost established for a non-weighted student) is increased by a multiplier, or index, for special needs children and for such high-cost education programs as vocational programs.
- Dollar allocations are increased for districts that have a "higher cost of services." This is usually known as *municipal overburden*.

- Categorical funds are provided for special "state-interest" programs: program enhancement, new programs, rules and regulations imposed on school districts, and education research.
- Sufficient state funds are provided for facilities and transportation services.
- State funds are distributed on the basis of weighted pupil units.

Five major models exist for determining adequacy, each of which we explain briefly.

Normative Data Model. This is probably the least complex approach that states use to establish an adequate education. In using this approach, the state first examines expenditures in other states and simply uses the average of those data to establish the base student cost for one non-weighted student. This expenditure is usually in the range of $5,000 to $6,000. The total number of students is then increased by appropriate indices or weightings to obtain the total weighted pupil units. The total of WPUs is multiplied by the base student cost to establish the total obligation of the state. The money is then distributed to each school district based on the number of WPUs in each district.

Another approach in using normative data is to examine the national average expenditure per non-weighted pupil and to use that average to establish the base non-weighted student cost for one student. This base cost is then increased by appropriate indices or weightings.

Using normative data is not applicable to establishing adequacy in the areas of facilities and transportation.

These areas are unique to each state, and expenditures cannot be based on averages of other states. Expenditures should be based on actual need for the total state and the current status of facilities.

Desired Results Model. The desired results model (often called the output model) is based on two assumptions: first, that a set of objectives for public schools can be established and, second, that it is possible to determine the cost for achieving those objectives. This is far more complex than most legislators believe it to be. Nevertheless, it has been used, most recently in Ohio. In a series of steps, officials:

1. Determine a set of objectives to be achieved that can be measured, primarily by tests (achievement levels) or by data analysis (graduation rates).
2. Identify school districts within the state that achieve the objectives.
3. Compute the average expenditure in those districts for a non-weighted fourth-grade student.
4. Establish this average as the base student cost.
5. Augment the cost of educating students in special programs with a system of weightings or indices.
6. Compute the total WPUs needed to be funded and multiply that figure by the student base cost to obtain the required state revenue.
7. Adjust the school finance formula for regional cost-of-living factors or municipal overburden.

In addition to funding the required results, the state would have separate funds for facilities, transportation, and categorically funded programs that are in the state's interest. The desired results model has recently been used in Ohio, Mississippi, New Hampshire, and several other states. However, in none of these states have legislators provided adequate funds to achieve the desired objectives.

The difficulty with this approach is that legislatures wish to obtain high results but are not willing to provide the money needed to achieve them. Going to the Moon "on the cheap" is a fairly common practice in most states when it comes to adequate funds for public education. The excuse often used is that they should not "throw money" at education. Since we have never done that, it might be wise to try it once.

Resource Model. Under the resource model, the state establishes a program of education services it wishes to provide and then computes the cost of implementing it. This is referred to as an "input model." The system requires that a large number of decisions be made prior to computing the base student cost. Examples include:

- What is the class size?
- What personnel salaries should be used?
- What is the length of the school year?
- What are the indices (weightings) to be used?
- How much technology is involved?

Usually a panel of school experts establishes a prototype school to compute the cost of an adequate education program. Each component of the school (salaries, books, utilities, technology, and so on) contributes to the total cost.

The resource model approach has been used in Wyoming under the guidance of James W. Guthrie and Richard Rothstein. A panel of experts made professional judgments as to what elements constitute an "adequate" school and then computed the cost of the elements. By adding the costs of each element, the panel obtained the total cost required to provide an adequate education program.

Critics of the resource model claim that professional judgment is not always stable, that the system is not always accurate, and that the system is not directly related to results. Nevertheless, the system does provide the state with a basis to determine the total cost required by controlling the elements of a prototype adequate school. Therefore it is generally favored by state legislators who wish to provide minimum education resources.

Often the resource model perpetuates the notion that equal per pupil expenditure is all that is needed to provide adequacy. However, a large number of children require special services that are not accounted for in the resource model. Therefore it is important that weightings or indices be used as a part of this model.

Education Priority Model. The education priority model is used by states that wish to control expenditures. First the state determines how much money the state believes it can afford for education. Then it places the burden on local districts to provide adequacy.

The education priority model affords legislators the freedom to establish extremely inadequate conditions (making education a low priority) and to place the burden on local districts to finance adequacy. This is, of course, a tremendous disadvantage to low-wealth school districts. High-wealth districts can easily provide additional funds by taxing themselves at relatively low levels.

Education affordability is a relative term, subject to the value placed on education by the legislature of the state. It is defined by politics and fiscal factors. In such states, the courts generally have ruled the system to be unconstitutional because it places unequal burdens on school districts. Low-wealth districts cannot supplement state funds as can high-wealth districts. Therefore the courts in such states impose a more realistic value on education and, thereby, the need for increased state support.

Funding strategies based on the education priority model worked well in previous decades. However, the model is so flawed that now it is nearly extinct. It should have died many years ago.

Econometric Model. The econometric model is generally the most expensive of the five models. It establishes large indices for a number of student characteristics. Its application demands lengthy and expensive research, as well as large amounts of new money. Conclusions obtained through the use of this model are controversial.

The econometric model establishes adequacy as a more comprehensive set of education services than those established by the other models. It gives consideration to many factors:

- Extra staff for extended and remedial services.
- Teacher training activities.

- School improvement efforts.
- Parental education programs.
- School readiness services.
- Safety and school climate programs.
- Indices for such sociological conditions as poverty, high risk, low income, disabilities, limited English proficiency, and special needs.

The model also factors in indices for economic conditions, such as a cost of living or labor market index, economy of scale as measured by school district size, and property values and assessed valuations.

Economists who pursue the econometric model are attempting to construct a "cost function" for the state's education system. The cost function is the money required to achieve a certain level of results with appropriate consideration given to different demographic characteristics of students and schools.

Using complicated mathematical formulae, the model establishes how much the state must spend for school districts with the state's average demographics to achieve at average performance levels. The formulae also can be used to establish the required funds to have these school districts achieve above the average state levels of performance. The higher the desired levels of performance, the greater the money needed to achieve them.

The model produces two numbers:

- The expenditure level needed to produce certain results in the "average" or "typical" districts, and
- The cost adjustments for producing these same results in school districts with non-average demographics.

The amount needed to produce average results would constitute the "foundation program." Districts with atypical demographics would receive more or less than the foundation program as determined by the variance of their demographics from the state average.

The goal of this model is similar to the desired results model, except that it gives consideration to many more sociological and economic factors. If the system can become more effective in predicting expenditures needed to obtain certain results by various demographic groups, the state would know how much money is needed in each school to obtain those results. Currently we have not yet reached that level of sophistication with this or any other model.

A Model Program for Adequacy

Recently, several states have attempted to establish a model adequacy school finance program. Resistance has come mainly from high-wealth school districts. For example, in New Hampshire it is especially strong from such property-rich cities as Portsmouth (Jiminez 2000). The same reaction has occurred in Vermont. As reported in *Forbes*:

> This shift in funding has evidently not been accompanied by a gain in educational results. "The good districts get worse, and the others don't get any better," says Dartmouth college professor William Fischel. "They have made education worse on average." (McMenamin 1999, p. 102)

Much of the reaction is based on emotion and strong resistance to an increase in taxes. It has little to do with education quality and fairness.

A model school finance program in any state where adequacy has not been established will require an increase in taxes. The logic seems clear: If the financial support is not adequate, then additional revenue is needed.

Following are the elements of an adequate financial program for public education in any state:

1. A foundation program that would provide each non-weighted student $5,500 to $6,000. This figure is established by using normative data and studies conducted by other school finance experts, such as James Gutherie and John Augenblick (Viadero 1999). This is a sufficient "base student cost" for most states.

2. The base student cost is increased each year by the cost-of-living index.

3. The base student cost is increased by a system of weightings or indices for the following:
   - Higher cost levels of education (such as high school).
   - Higher cost programs (such as vocational programs).
   - Students with disabilities.
   - Students who are gifted.
   - Students who live in poverty conditions.
   - Students who have special needs, for example, girls who are pregnant.

4. The base student cost is adjusted in accordance with the purchasing power of various regions. This is often called "cost of doing business," "municipal overburden," or "labor market index."

These four provisions constitute the elements of an adequate program of education services. In addition, the state also must provide adequacy in facilities and transportation. To do so the state should:

1. Implement a statewide building program funded 100% by state funds. Building priorities would be established based on need by a state commission on school facilities.
2. Establish a program of 100% funding for transportation. Routes established by local districts would have to comply with statewide criteria for both regular routes and activity routes.

Providing adequacy in facilities, transportation, and education services would require additional taxes at the state level in nearly all states. Some states may wish to go beyond these three components and establish categorical funding to promote the state's interests. These would include:

- State rules and regulations related to accountability structures.
- Character education programs.
- Staff development opportunities.
- Research activities.
- Retirement benefits.

The most important question before the state legislature is: How does the state fund education, especially an adequate education? A model funding program consists of these elements:

- *Adequacy of revenue.* The system is based on the entire wealth of the state and not on the accident of geography.

- *Ability to be understood.* The school finance program should be relatively easy to understand.
- *Protection from administrative manipulation.* School funds should be protected from manipulations by legislators or financial officers.
- *Basis in current requirements.* The funding system should keep current with changing conditions and the introduction of new requirements.
- *Equity.* The finance program should provide an equitable distribution of funds to all districts based on need, the foundation program, plus weightings.

To obtain sufficient revenue, the state should establish state-level taxes. Some states may wish to implement a plan that shares the cost between the state and local districts. The state, however, should take responsibility for at least 90% of the funding.

Local districts may wish to tax themselves at a higher level than the state-imposed tax. They should be permitted to do so and to keep the entire collected revenue.

Adequacy for public education has never been established, nor have we ever thrown money at schools. It would be a great moral act if we did it just once. In the absence of doing that, however, it is in our national interest to establish an education system that can adequately educate our young people. However, it does require courage and duty from state legislators.

We conclude with a statement made by Percy E. Burrup and his colleagues in *Financing Education in a Climate of Change* (1999, p. 59):

> As expensive as public education may be, the cost
> to society of not educating people is much higher.

The detrimental effect of illiteracy on employment, on military capability, and on the size of welfare and relief rolls is strong evidence of the costliness of permitting people to remain uneducated.

Financing education at less than an adequate level is poor economy. With such a large investment in buildings and facilities, the 50 states must provide enough revenue to protect that investment and to achieve the best possible education for all their youth, regardless of their place of residence, the wealth of their parents, or the wealth of their school district.

There is no need to say more.

References

Burrup, Percy E., et al. *Financing Education in a Climate of Change*. Needham Heights, Mass.: Allyn & Bacon, 1999.

Jiminez, Ralph. *Boston Globe*, 2 January 2000, p. 1.

Ludlow, Randy. "Well-Off Schools May Pay for Reform." *Cincinnati Post*, 13 May 2000, p. 1.

McMenamin, Brigid. "Robin Hood Doesn't Approve." *Forbes*, 13 December 1999, p. 102.

Viadero, Debra. "How Much Is Enough?" *Education Week*, 29 September 1999, pp. 28-30.

Recent Books Published by the Phi Delta Kappa Educational Foundation

Readings on Leadership in Education
From the Archives of Phi Delta Kappa International
Trade paperback. $22 (PDK members, $16.50)

Profiles of Leadership in Education
Mark F. Goldberg
Trade paperback. $22 (PDK members, $16.50)

Quest for Truth:
Scientific Progress and Religious Beliefs
Mano Singham
Trade paperback. $22 (PDK members, $16.50)

Education in the United Kingdom and Ireland
James E. Green
Trade paperback. $15 (PDK members, $12)

American Education in the 21st Century
Dan H. Wishnietsky
Trade paperback. $22 (PDK members, $16.50)

Use Order Form on Next Page
Or Phone 1-800-766-1156

A processing charge is added to all orders.
Prices are subject to change without notice.

Complete online catalog at http://www.pdkintl.org

Order Form